PRONUNCIATION GUIDE: KIMBUNDU TO ENGLISH

KIMBUNDU	PRONUNCIATION	ENGLISH
SOBA	SUH-BAH	TRADITIONAL RULER
PANGUEAMI	PAN-GOO-EE-AH-MEE	BROTHER
XIKOLA	SEE-KOH-LAH	SCHOOL
KUHOKA	KOO-HOO-KAH	TIRED
MUKUA-MBELE	MOO-KOO-AH EM-BAY-LAY	HELPERS
NJINGA	N-JIN-GAH	
NGOLA	N-GOH-LAH	
NDONGO	N-DON-GOH	
MBANDI	MBAH-DEE	
KILUANJI	KEE-LOO-AHN-JEE	
MATAMBA	MAH-TAH-MBAH	

SOFT "J" AS IN MEASURE

The Kimbundu alphabet comprises 26 letters:
- Five vowels: a, e, i, o, u
- Two soft consonants: y, w
- Nineteen consonants: b, d, f, h, j, k, l, m, n, s, t, v, x, z, bh, ng, ny, ph, th

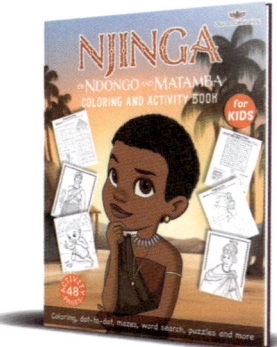

Our accompanying **Njinga of Ndongo and Matamba** coloring and activity book provides additional learning opportunities and engaging activities for further enrichment.

OTHER BOOKS IN THE "OUR ANCESTORIES" LINEUP

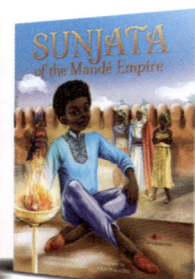

VISIT US AT OUR-ANCESTORIES.COM
to get free resources, lesson plans, our African History Digital Workbook, and the other books in the Our Ancestories series.

This Book Belongs To:

_____

Copyright © 2021 Our Ancestories

Map design by Mats Wedin
Book design by Dania Zafar
Research assistance by Marianela Parodi
Edited by Mary Blake, Shamontiel Vaughn, and Brooke Vitale
Pronunciations by Jonilson Salvador

All rights reserved. No part of this publication may be reproduced, distributed, or transmitted in any form or by any means, including photocopying, recording, or other electronic or mechanical methods, without the prior written permission of the publisher, except in the case of brief quotations embodied in critical reviews and certain other noncommercial uses permitted by copyright law.

ISBN: 978-1-7771179-5-5 (Hardcover)

Second printing edition 2023

www.our-ancestories.com

NJINGA
OF NDONGO AND MATAMBA

WRITTEN BY
EKIUWA AIRE

ILLUSTRATED BY
NATALIA POPOVA

Over 400 years ago, in what is now Angola, a baby girl was born. She was the daughter of the *soba* (the traditional ruler). He was called Mbandi Kiluanji, and he was of the Kimbundu people of Ndongo.

But something was wrong! During the baby's birth, a cord around her neck made it hard for her to breathe.

The nurse gently wrapped the baby in soft cloths and took her to the *soba*. "The baby is dying," she explained tearfully.

Taking the silent baby, *Soba* Kiluanji looked carefully into her tiny face. There was strength in her; he was sure of it. He did not want his daughter to die. He did not even know her yet, but already he loved her dearly. What could he do? *Perhaps I could breathe for her,* he thought.

Drawing a deep breath, the *soba* covered the baby's mouth and nose with his own mouth. Then he gently blew air into her lungs.

He looked again at her face. Still no crying. No breathing. But yet, he saw her strength. She wanted to live.

Taking another deep breath, he again carefully filled her lungs.

Again and again, *Soba* Kiluanji breathed for his daughter. He would not give up.

Finally, the baby cried ... and moved. She was alive!

The *soba* laughed with delight.

"I was certain she was lost, but you have breathed life back into her!" exclaimed the nurse.

The nurse carried the baby to her mother. "Here is your beautiful baby," she told her. "She has survived a difficult birth. She will grow up to do great things."

The story of the ruler's exceptional daughter quickly spread. Soon, it reached the ears of Mbandi, her *pangueami* (brother).

But what is so great about her? Mbandi wondered. She was only a baby and not even a boy! Everyone knew that the firstborn son was the most important child!

She is not special, he thought.

The baby was named Njinga (twist) Mbandi because of her difficult birth.

She was strong, healthy, active, and bright. She captured her father's heart from the very beginning. *Soba* Kiluanji loved to play with Njinga.

When she was old enough, he sent her to *xikola* (school) because he wanted her to learn to read and write in Portuguese. The Ndongo kingdom often had dealings with the government of the European country of Portugal.

Mbandi was not happy. "School is not for girls," he said.

The *soba* did not listen to him. "Your sister is quite smart," he said. "She will go to school with you."

One day, when Njinga was seven, her teacher (a Portuguese missionary) asked a question. "Do you know how to recite your numbers in Portuguese?"

"Of course," answered Njinga. "*Zero, um, dois, três...*"

Njinga kept going. Just as she passed the number twelve, Mbandi interrupted her.

"The teacher has only taught us up to the number ten," he said. "How do you know these other numbers?"

"I studied at home," answered Njinga. "I can go all the way to one hundred!"

The teacher laughed and later reported the story to the *soba*. "My, you are clever, Njinga," he said.

Mbandi scowled. *It isn't fair. She's just showing off! Njinga should not be allowed in school!*

A few years later, Njinga's father was crowned the *ngola* (king) of Ndongo. He started to invite Njinga to join him in attending to the business of the kingdom. This made Mbandi even more unhappy.

Njinga watched eagerly as her father went about his duties.

When she was old enough, the *ngola* even took Njinga to war. "Why do you bring her, Father?" asked Mbandi. "She can do nothing. She's a waste of time."

But *Ngola* Kiluanji disagreed. "As an infant, she fought to live. She is a fighter."

"I don't see anything special about her," objected Mbandi. "She's just a girl."

Njinga listened closely as her father talked with other rulers or made military plans. She learned everything she could. It became clear that she not only breathed her father's breath but also shared his talent for leadership. As time passed, Portugal made more rules for the people of the kingdom. *Ngola* Kiluanji fought back for many years.

The constant fighting made him very sad and *kuhoka* (tired).

In 1617, *Ngola* Mbandi Kiluanji joined the ancestors.

Mbandi became the new *ngola*. Some in the kingdom were unhappy with *Ngola* Mbandi's rule. He was cruel, bitter, and listened to no one. *He has always resented me,* thought Njinga, *and now he is powerful. I will not be welcome in his kingdom.*

Njinga knew that she must leave Ndongo.

Helped by her faithful *mukua-mbele* (helpers),
Njinga ran away to a nearby kingdom of Matamba.

Things did not go well for the Ndongo kingdom under *Ngola* Mbandi's rule. The Portuguese government threatened to take over, demanding riches and slaves from among the people.

Ngola Mbandi did not know what to do. He didn't like it at all, but he had to admit that he needed his sister.

Njinga, because she spoke Portuguese, was the only person who might talk with the Portuguese and convince them to treat the Ndongo kingdom fairly. So, Mbandi swallowed his pride and sent for her.

Njinga did not trust her brother. *It may only be a trick so that he can hurt me*, she thought. But she knew that her people needed her help. Despite the danger, she decided to return.

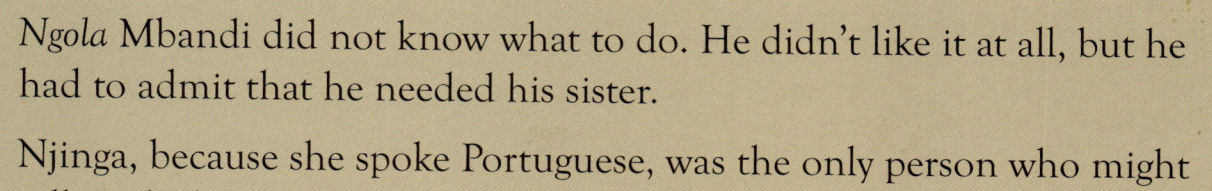

Njinga went to Luanda, in the heart of the Ndongo kingdom, to see the Portuguese governor, Dom João Correia de Sousa. There, she expected to be treated as an equal.

But de Sousa sat in a grand chair and directed her to sit on the floor. This was to let everyone know that Njinga was not nearly as important as he was.

It did not work. When Njinga spoke to her *mukua-mbele* (helpers), one of them dropped down to his hands and knees, creating a proper chair for her. On his back, Njinga sat like a queen on her throne, looking the governor straight in the eyes.

Njinga's mission was a success! She outsmarted the governor, convincing him to be kinder to her people.

Ngola Mbandi was not so lucky; he lost control of his kingdom. He ran away to a small island on the Kwanza River where he died of mysterious circumstances.

Njinga Mbandi became queen, just as her nurse and her father had imagined many years before.

Queen Njinga was a strong ruler. She worked hard to keep her people safe and free. She defended them from the Portuguese and from all who threatened them.

In time, however, threats against the Ndongo became too great for the people. The land was no longer safe. *Ngola* Njinga fought to conquer the Kingdom of Matamba and moved her people there. Now she was queen of two united kingdoms.

Despite the difficulties she faced, Njinga Mbandi remained queen for many years. Her brother was wrong. Njinga was not "just a girl." She was a smart ruler, a gifted queen, and a brave warrior. To this very day, she is remembered as the determined and courageous Queen Njinga of Ndongo and Matamba.

Just the Facts

The Ndongo and Matamba Kingdoms

- Angola is the seventh-largest country in Africa. Africa is a continent. The world contains seven continents.

- The kingdom of Ndongo was located in what is now called Angola. The kingdom of Matamba was located in what is now called the Democratic Republic of Congo.

- The language spoken by the Ndongo people was **Kimbundu**. This is the language used for some phrases in this story!

- Angola's name comes from the Ndongo people's word for king: *Ngola*.

- The Portuguese were the first Europeans to come to Angola. The Portuguese explorer, Diogo Cao, arrived in 1484.

- It was not easy to be a ruler over Ndongo. The kingdom faced multiple problems.

    While some Portuguese wanted to help Ndongo's people, others (including some among the government) wanted to take their land and make them slaves.

    The Kingdom of Kongo threatened to take over Ndongo and demanded riches in return for safety and peace. Kongo also took slaves from neighboring kingdoms; some they kept, and others were sold to the Portuguese.

    The Imbangala were a warrior group that threatened to topple other kingdoms and set up their own. Njinga married their chief because she wanted to achieve peace with the group. The Imbangala helped Njinga ascend to power in Matamba but later betrayed her, attacking Matamba.

- After Njinga's death, Portugal did finally take over Angola, and Angola did not again win its independence until many years later.

- Today, Angola is an important country and economy in Africa. Many of the world's diamonds come from Angola, and Angola is also a big oil producer.

Just the Facts
Njinga of Ndongo and Matamba

- Njinga was born around the year 1581 and died around 1663. She lived for about 82 years.

- The name Njinga is derived from the Kimbundu verb *kujinga*, meaning "to twist or turn."

- During Njinga's life, her land and people faced being taken over by Europeans, especially Portuguese. Njinga's leadership allowed Angola to avoid such conquests during her lifetime.

- Njinga became Queen of Ndongo in 1623, at about age 42.

- As queen, Njinga promptly declared to the world that Angola was a free and independent country.

- Sometime after Njinga became queen, the Portuguese broke the agreement that they had made with her. They attacked Ndongo, forcing Njinga to escape (as she had done early in her brother's reign) to Matamba.

- Njinga married the chief of the warrior group Imbangala. (In many cultures throughout history, marriage was often used to create political partnerships.) Njinga was able to use the Imbangala warriors to conquer Matamba and become queen. But the Imbangala later abandoned their loyalty to Njinga and attacked Matamba, and Njinga had to go into hiding (exile).

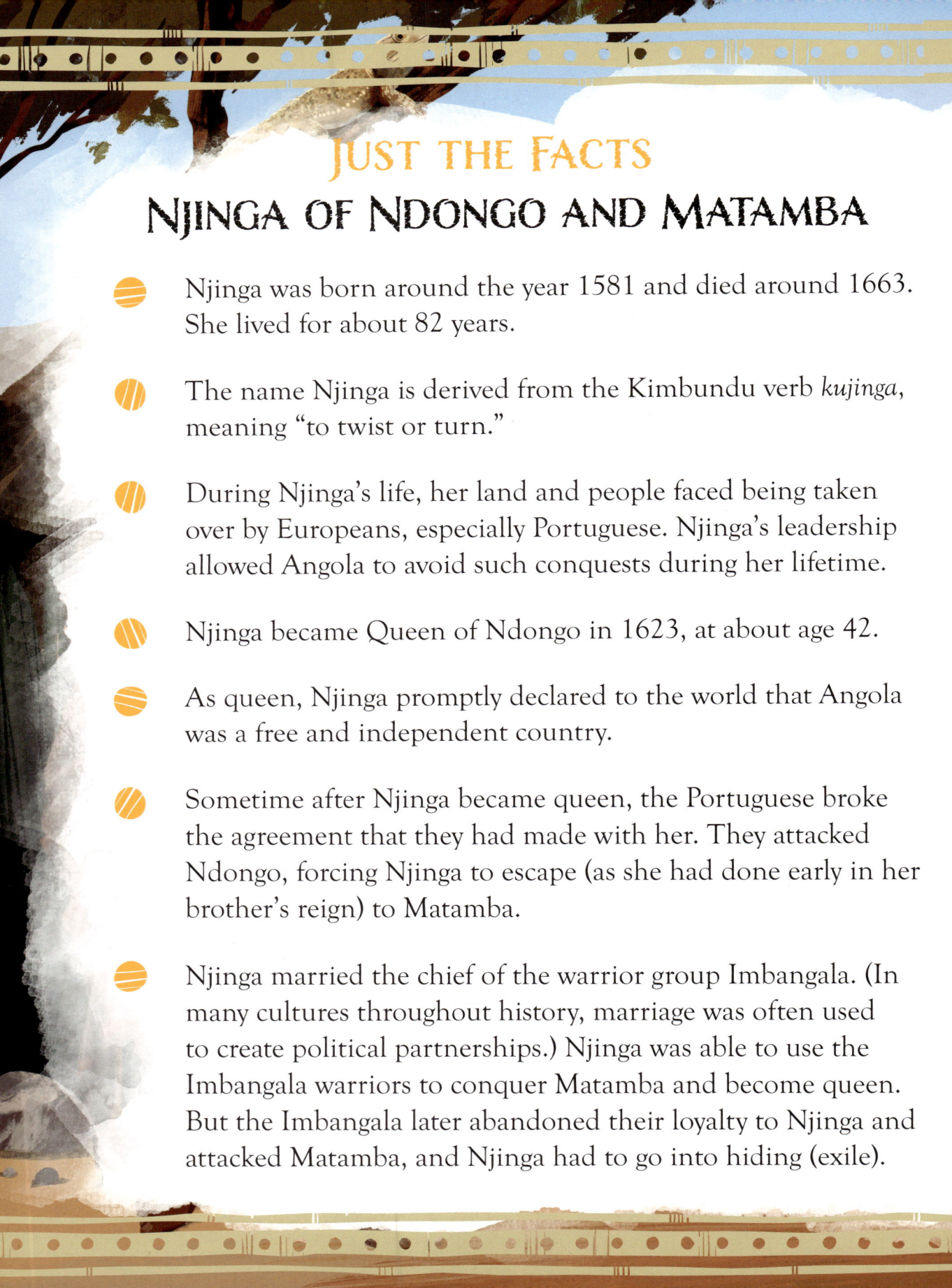

- Since so many remained loyal to her, Njinga was able to lead even from exile. She commanded warriors in battle against the Portuguese. At the same time, she made friends with the Dutch (other European people present in Africa) to persuade them in her cause against Portugal. She demonstrated exceptional abilities both militarily and politically.

- Queen Njinga Mbande is known by many different names, including both Kimbundu and Portuguese names, alternate spellings, and various honorifics. Common spellings found in Portuguese and English sources include Nzinga, Nzingha, Njinga, and Njingha. In colonial documentation, including her own manuscripts, her name was also spelled Jinga, Ginga, Zinga, Zingua, Zhinga, and Singa. She was also known by her Christian name, Ana de Sousa.

- Queen Njinga was a powerful figure in African history who inspired others to fight for independence. She was known for her strength, bravery, and intelligence. She was also a complex character with many different traits and motivations.

- Njinga fought for the good of her country and people against Portuguese colonization and the slave trade. She protected escaped slaves, but at other times, she also traded people as slaves to acquire resources like weapons or luxuries.

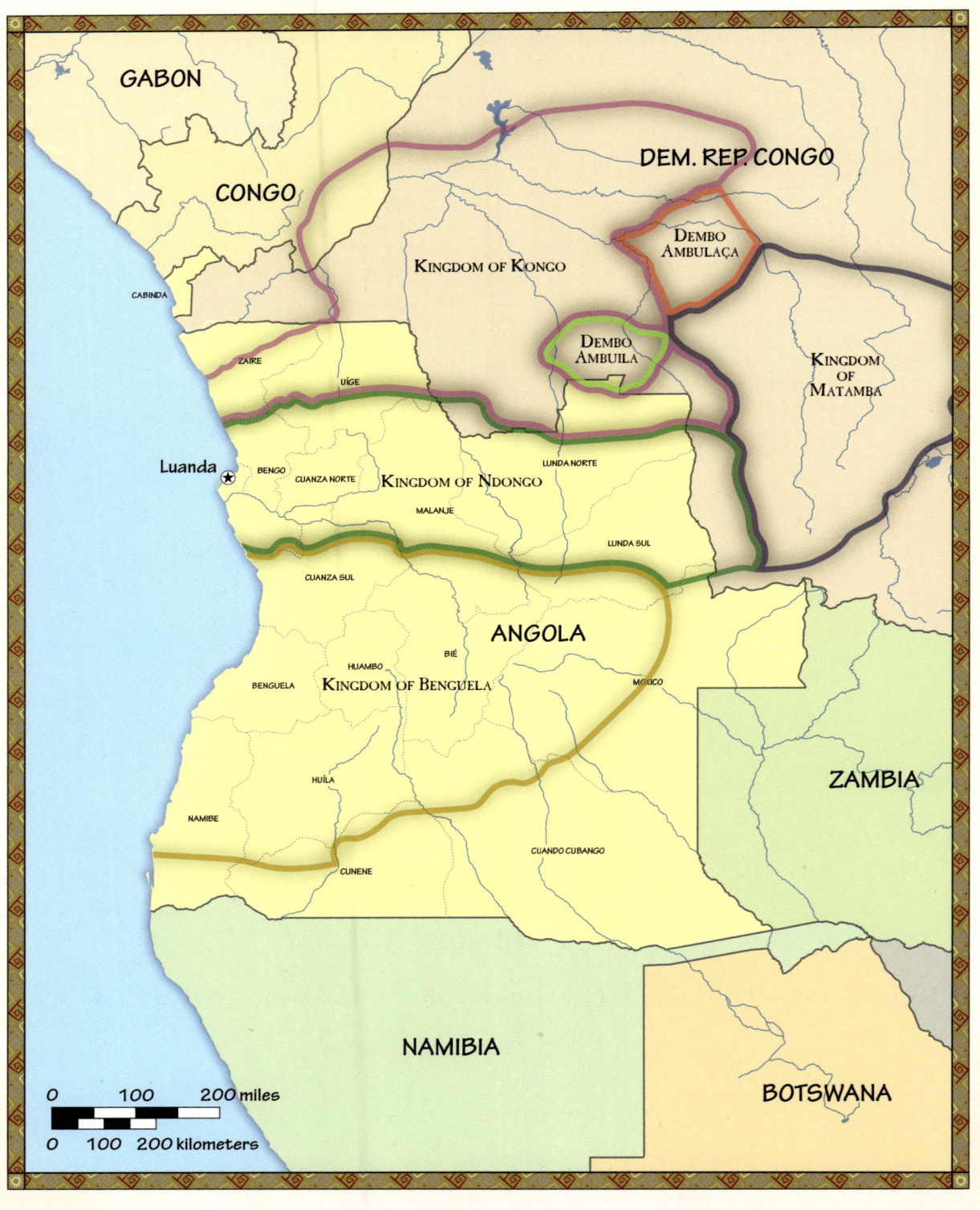

References

- Barrett-Graves, D., Carney, J., Kennedy, G., Levin, C., & Spellman, W. M. Witham, S. (2000). *Extraordinary Women of the Medieval and Renaissance World: A Biographical Dictionary.*
- Collelo, T. (1991). *Angola: A country study.* U.S. G.P.O.
- Coquery-Vidrovitch, C., & Raps, B. G. (1997). *African women.*
- Heywood, L. (2017). *Njinga of Angola: Africa's Warrior Queen.* Harvard University Press.
- Landers, J. G., & Robinson, B. M. (Eds.). (2006). *Slaves, Subjects, and Subversives: Blacks in Colonial Latin America.* University of New Mexico Press.
- Miller, J. C. (1975). *Nzinga of Matamba in a New Perspective.* The Journal of African History, 16(2), 201-216.
- Smith, C. A. (2005). *Market Women: Black Women Entrepreneurs: Past, Present, and Future.* Praeger Publishers.
- Stapleton, T. J. (2011). *Njinga Mbande, Queen of Ndongo and Matamba (ca. 1583–1663).*
- UNESCO. (2014). *Njinga Mbandi: Queen of Ndongo and Matamba.* UNESCO.

Subject Matter Expert Consulted

- Domingos Bengo (Academic researcher)

ABOUT THE AUTHOR

Ekiuwa Aire is an award-winning author and speaker born and raised in Benin City, Edo, Nigeria. She is passionate about sharing positive stories on African history with children.

She lives with her husband and two daughters in Ontario, Canada.

ABOUT THE ILLUSTRATOR

Natalia Popova studied visual arts and illustration at Moscow State University. After graduation, she became a full-time freelance artist specializing in character designs, commercials, and book illustrations. She currently lives in Bali near the ocean.